D0707534

THE
LATINX
POETRY
PROJECT

By **ALEGRIA** PUBLISHING

Ordering Information:
Quantity sales. Special discounts are available on quantity
purchases by corporations, associations, and others. For
details, contact the publisher at
davina@alegriamagazine.com

Orders by U.S. trade bookstores and wholesalers. Please
contact Big Distribution:
www.ingramspark.com

Printed in the United States of America.

Library of Congress Control Number: 2020906202

PUBLISHER'S NOTE

Throughout the process of bringing The LatinX Poetry Project to life, my heart has been filled with indescribable joy.

The idea for this magical creative endeavor came to me as I was preparing to publish If Love Had a Name, my very own poetry collection. As you may know, writing a book can often be a solitary journey.

I was ready for a collective project. On this lonely road, driven by individualistic creativity, nothing is more welcome than the spirit of community

As a poet myself, I find inspiration by soaking in the words of fellow poets. While they keep this beautiful art form alive, through artistic collaborations and new digital possibilities, they also enlighten us with their raw and soulful work.

To this day, the publishing industry continues to underrepresent diverse writers and, as a result, deny readers the power and beauty of necessary voices. It is my hope that through an inclusive collection like this, we can amplify relevant cultural narratives and shine a light on the rich humanity contained within our stories.

There are those that would have us believe LatinX poets are extinct or on their way to becoming irrelevant. Nothing is further from the truth. We are very much alive and we are everywhere.

Across the globe, our lives are the very definition of magical realism. We inherited poetry –carried from our ancestors' tongues into the DNA of every generation to follow. It was this longing, this passionate commitment to find new LatinX poets and storytellers, that moved me to create this sacred space.

First, my company, ALEGRIA Media and Publishing, ran a poetry contest. We opened it to anyone with a desire to talk about immigration, social justice and feminism today. I never imagined such an incredible response. Hundreds of poems were received and I personally read each and every one, literally crying tears of joy. I had found my tribe. I was not alone. Thank you for showing up. Thank you for being so vulnerable - for having the courage to share your heart with all of us.

I hope you enjoy The Latinx Poetry Project. Born out of a love for poetry and poets, it brings together more than 45 new LatinX voices.

It is my dream for this launch to skip like a stone across the water's surface, creating an ever-widening ripple effect, reflecting the magnitude of our human potential. May it be the beginning of creative collaborations that carry a lasting impact.

By purchasing this book, you are supporting LatinX artists and storytellers.

Please check **@alegriamagazine** for new and upcoming LatinX books & magazines.

Much ALEGRÍA & Poesía Always,

Davina Ferreira

davina@alegriamagazine.com
www.davinaferreira.com
IG @ davifalegria

THEY CALL ME CHISMOSA

They call me chismosa or
gossiping woman
because I have stories
instead of manners
dreams instead of children

"chismooooossaaaaaa"

the word casts a spell
around itself
breaks the silence of the
night with a sharpened
machete
opposite of a chismosa:
a muñeca
the porcelain painted
doll in the dining room
cupboard
a girl with lips sealed
wso tight
she woke up one day and
forgot how to speak
I however, was born
screaming
& never quite learned how
to stop
I escaped from my silicone
box long ago
and never could
go back
they call me chismosa
and I say
"Thank you, I have
dedicated years to
the craft."

If I had a nickel for every
time a man spoke over me
I could even out the
wage gap
I could rent a recording
studio and start my own
chismosa podcast
I could buy out all the
rows of plastic girls in
the store aisle
and crack them open
& when news breaks
that another Maria is
kidnapped in my town

I will not sit still
on a shelf
I will buy a megaphone
open the chamber of mouth
spit the slicked saliva
gasoline into the ether
&
set the city ablaze
before silence swallows
another
chismosa you call me
because you know you
cannot kill a woman
with more
language than fear
because you know a mouth
with a story,
and the nerve to tell it,
lives
forever.

By: Angelica Maria Aguilera

BURIED

By: Elizabeth Quintal

Heavy.
Suffocating.
Lungs filled with air
but unable to release.
Bricks, not tied to
your feet,
Stacked bit by bit on
your shoulders as you
sink
deeper into the
ground.

How else will they
build the wall
but on top of you
And from underneath
the earth you
look up to see less and
less blue sky.
The dirt and mud and
clay coat you,
Thick, damp, cool
remaking you.
They will pat
themselves on the back.
Will say it wasn't
intentional or even
personal,
and most certainly not
racist.
A simple by product of
what needed to happen.
You know, for the
economy,
for security,

for states' rights,
for a way of life,
for lower taxes,
or maybe they are
illegal or MS13 and
all that.

'Til that morning in
May, when arms stretch
beyond the possible
and fingers sprout
through the cracks,
break through
concrete,
rupture bricks.
And a little girl,
her long black hair
braided,
plucks you up and
blows.

You are the million
wishes and the roots of
who she is.
And now you travel
below the surface and
through the air.

Every weed I see
is a reminder that,
brick by brick,
you can bury me
but never shatter my
lungs
or break my wings.

NOT INTENDED FOR DISPLAY

By: Elizabeth Quintal

I am the brown earth.

The dirt,
the fertile soil.

But I need the blue,
the waters deep and
sweet and sour too.

That's how I form the
clay and create
the shapes of being
and laughter, of
ache and love—of
first day of school
memories,
the touch of grass
tickling toes, days
filled with slides
and swings, hand in
hand walking,
hips swaying to
beats, smells of mole,
a squeeze of lime, how
to use a molcajete, and
that
first bite of chocolate
chip cookie.

Until the day you
smash it
with your hammer or
AK-47.

Collect the shards,
display them in your
museums,
call them ethnic,
lay your head on your
pillow,
and sleep.

So proud
with yourself.

FREEDOM TASTES

Freedom tastes like a meal of fresh and rotten, all at the same time. Making the palate uncomfortable, but opening your taste buds to the complexity and the reality of it all.

Not all are able to sit through this uncomfortable meal. It is more than a moment, it is an exercise in the mind, and opening up to our capacity to feel. To be present in the realities and complexities that go beyond just mine.

The choice to sit here was costly for many who came before us. Blood, gas baths, land, culture, language, and dignity among the payments not willingly taken up. All things I cannot fathom, or take for granted, as I sit in the dark.

I will sit at this table over and over again. I will taste, listen, and mourn. Because right in the middle of darkness, the light of truth is always born. The moon shines through the darkness that could not extinguish its light.

Freedom tastes bittersweet all at the same time.

By: Alma Cardenas

MIJA HIT MY EARS ALMOST AS MUCH AS MY NAME

By: Christiana Castillo

Mija is my darling,
a blessing passed,
the water
filling
a cactus

Mija is a life force,
The leftovers
filling
your insides

Mija is the Chicana
down the street
and the baby
laughing
in the crib

Mija is praying,
holding her hands
like Guadalupe

Mija is the warmth
from a prayer candle
The one that will
always
get lit again
Mija is the braid
from abuela

running down
my back
Mija is the warm comal
and the avocado in
my tortilla
Mija is keeping us full

Mija is the brown girl
who is younger than
you and helped you
at the bodega

Mija is your tías,
but not your real tías,
daughter

Mija is filling bee
stings
with dirt

Mija is planting
marigolds out back
Mija is the sound of
home
Mija is my name too
Mija is for the brown
girls.

AZTEC SHRINE

When I was young
I learned soy
Mexicana.
I learned that mi familia
es fuerte.
Filled with women
that have spirits
entangled in their hair,
we chose
to believe that we came
from the
Aztec people.

So when I learned that my
body
and my mind
were to be considered
temples
and
shrines,
I considered mine
to be their
pyramids,
golden with vines
and life
crawling throughout.
I was beautiful.

Other people
found me
beautiful too.
Then chaos
entered my mind
and I was not young

By: Christiana Castillo

and colonizers
came and
went.
They cast
new demons,
demons I
could not pray away.

So how do I
resurrect
my own collapse
when I
envisioned myself
after a great
and powerful
people?

People that
lost their homes,
their religions,
and civilization,
they
crumble.

When my mind shifts
and manipulation
occurs,
I am crumbling
and spiraling.

The Aztecs ruled for
about 100 years,
400 less than

most great
civilizations.
Only to be
taken over by people
who did not
belong.
Authenticity is:
remember more than
assimilation.

I am not waiting
for a white god
to save me.
I am not waiting
for a new shrine.
I survived.

I will sacrifice you
to the gods
while I am in
an abundance of
turquoise.
You will be looking
up from badlands.

My shrine is gold.
It's hundreds of
steps.
The only sacrifices
I make now are
for me,
I survived.

COMPLIMENTS: VEILED SCRUTINY

By: Ariel Vidal

Forgive them Father,
for they know not
what they do.
They say things
without stopping to
think
about the meaning.

"You're prettier with
makeup on."
I'm prettier
without it.
It's just different.

"Take a page from
her book.
A lady should never
leave the house
without pressing her
clothes
or putting on a fresh
face of makeup.
Even going to the
supermarket,
a full face of makeup
is a must."
Excuse me?
I'm not a lady.
I'm me.

"You should wear
colors more;
you would look nicer."

It's no wonder why
I can't take a
compliment.
They're not given.
Everyone is so focused
on
everyone else fitting
their standard.

I'm not quiet about
self-esteem issues
and fluctuations.

I don't adhere to
your standard.
You don't get to
back up
your rude comments
as Gospel.

If you knew the Word
then you would
remember that
there is nothing
about makeup.
I put my best foot
forward

when I feel my best,
not when I'm adhering
to your standard.

I put my best
foot forward
when I'm not put
under a microscope.

"She's wearing
makeup for once.
Let's nag her
about how
that is the only way
to present yourself."

So much for
loving yourself
in the skin and image
God gave you, hm?
"A woman's got to
know her place."
You're worse than the
patriarchy.

Forgive them Father,
for they know not
what they do.

They don't see their
vanity,
insanity,
complimenting
fallacy.

Forgive them Father,
for they don't
understand
the pressure of always
having to
adhere to the
standards
of those who sold
their souls
for vanity.

Forgive them Father,
for they are hurting
people
without realizing it.

Forgive them Father,
for old people
never change.
They'd rather die
burning
and hurting people
than accept those who
think different.

Forgive them Father,
for they have strayed.
They won't change;
they'll die with
their vanity.
Forgive them.

WHERE I'M FROM

By: Ramona Ferreyra

Sewage in the heat.
Wet wooden homes.
Rain dropping on
leaves.

I am from the
edge where trash
accumulates. Forming
mounds and releasing
stench. It sits there
as if it read that New
York Times article
naming Mott Haven
the next frontier.

But few last here
because of the smell
in the summer.
Because of the rats
in the winter. They
don't take the time
to uncover my spot.
This place free of
YEEEERRRSSSS, free
of new beards and
trendy beers.

This small ledge
where I stand at times
staring at water that
seems unfamiliar. On
this ledge, I sometimes
admire the moon
asking la Diosa Luna
to let me see some
beauty in the murk.
Longing for the way
that water flirted
with greens and blues.

These hues so deep
that one coat of paint
would not do. But
this hue my heart
understood. A blue
familiar because
before being stripped
from the place that
eats the sun and spits
out platanos, my
spirit knew that we
would lose. But it is
so many blues...

RAMONA

There's a pang, one that
thumps to the rhythm of a
tambora. She feels that it
will come, around the same
time as the rain. And that
drum will be replaced por
un ceiling made of tin.

Drip
Drip
Drip

That's how the anger seeps.

She switched up her prayers
by the time they had that
second child. Around
the same time that the
mountain grew stubborn.
She no longer cared for
a companion. Instead she
prayed por el campo. Para
que su familia no sufriera
tanto. Years later that
prayer became canto.

Ojala que llueva café
en el campo.

By: Ramona Ferreyra

ALEGRIA PUBLISHING

BLISTERING FEET UNDER BLISTERING SUN

By: Fei Hernández

America is the only
gardener without
a backbone I know.
Picked immigrants,
planted them in

farms or white
people homes or
restaurants
or factories or
buses or McDonald

where their Brown
and Black hands
lifted the economy
from depression.

Picking, growing,
cleaning, scrubbing,
rotting, rearing,
cooking for you!
Yet ya'll call us
illegal?

When mami and I
immigrated to this
country,
she taught me little
things were big
things:

the garage where
concrete floor was
bed was actually
a mansion of
imagination where
mami was also my
father,

where Spanish was
The Bible that
erased all struggle
&
the nine-digit
branding me citizen
was non-existent.

I've always been
oblivious to my blue
skin or the third
eye
the alien people saw
in me
until opportunities
were
blank
like the social
security
number I couldn't
fill in
never turned in
like my vote in an
election.

But before my rage
lit a match and set a
nation on fire, mami
said:
Paciencia, it's the
spirit's way, my sky.
Growing up mami
never let my bare feet
touch

ground.

She knew friend's
brother's daughter's of
their sister's,
brother's friend's
whose daughter's
sisters

died with blistering
feet under a
blistering
sun crossing the
border. Mami taught me
how to swim.

It was her way of
erasing the bitter
taste of dead bodies
from water—
they call us
immigrants
wetbacks

because my people
never
lifted from the pits
of any body of water.
Fabis speak up! Talk
louder, mijo!

She didn't want
my voice to recede
to the sound of a
whisper
or become silent
like a statistic
in an elementary
school textbook.

Mami yelled at me
and flung a finger
to my face & said,
In your body, one
body, all will stand!

& yes ma
they do!

& we ain't
going anywhere.

We ain't going
anywhere!
WE. AIN'T. GOING.
ANYWHERE.

DRESSING MYSELF MAMI

By: Fei Hernández

This song is not an
analogy about my
mother's
miscarriage.

It's not about her guilt,
working strenuous
hours and leaving me
alone with grammar
equations.

This tale is not about
the man she wept for that
left us in a foreign
country
alone without syntactic

competency for a new
language.

This odyssey is not
about her clinic
abortion after the wind
mysteriously left her
impregnated with my
father's second child.

I had to do it amor. I
couldn't take care of
you and your brother
and me and me
in a new country all
alone.

This proclamation is
about how I pretend

myself to be a bearer
of children or
tatarabuela with a
long line of progeny.

These words are how
I document the way I
mourn for a rounder
belly
filled with a zygote
who will
live and become
toddler who will fill
the walls of my home
with laughter
and scribbles on the
floor that say: I love
you mami.

These couplets are
about my uterus
walls, how they open
and I glide out—how
every full

moon is a perpetual
flushing that won't
come back—
me slipping
from
me.

Sometimes, I wish
I could conjure my
dreams
into reality the same
way I write stories—

If I could, I would
script a uterus to glow
towards me,
halo, singing angels,
and all—
how I would reach for it
and stuff it
into my chest and
believe in God again—
from my chest
children would fly out
like doves. The crowd
would harmonize.

This obituary is about
how I want to be a
mother,
but a whole body is at
war with me.

Yet I don't know a
formula
to make me a better
daughter, though—
what a sinister balk
I am to unbury all of
mami's secrets
to create a telenovela
out of the trauma she
suffered, simply
to immortalize us in
a country that never
wanted us
remembered in the
fabric of its history.

Maybe I want to carry
the bricks lumped on
her shoulders
to know what it's like
to be a brick house, a

writer, anything but
a male-bodied cage.

I wear her heartbreak,
use her red lipstick,
and outline
my eyes with black
wings, like I'm not
already a funeral

all on my own wishing
I was wishing I was
woman enough.
I'll never be an Ama or
woman enough only an
aside.

But even on my
loneliest nights
typing tragic
vignettes,
even when I steal
from my own mother
without citation,
she places her arms
around my broad
shoulders and with
a wide
smile on her face
says:

Mi Vida, everything
that's mine
has always been
yours—
including the woman
inside of you.
Now, write us into
life,
take us to places
we've never existed.

CIEN AÑOS

By: Claudia Aparicio

Mmmmm...do you hear?

They are vibrating
throughout her body
Her gentle, rough
hands

Pecosas

Hermosas

With knowledge of
our antepasados
Inherited

Passed

Down

Caresses the leaves
of mi árbol de
naranja
Or was it of
mandarins?

I do remember the
chaos in body

My cells...stomach...
throat...skin

Not in harmony with
one another

Maybe because I was
outside with wet hair
The air infusing my
being

Or, maybe, possibly,
probably

Because I talked back

Simmering
Simmering

Simmering
Emeralds in a mad pool
Sacrificing
themselves
Tómatelo con miel,
hija
Sitting down, las dos

Talking about "cuando
tu papá era chico"

And I think that is
what made the knots in
my stomach hug each
other
P.S. It's OFelia and not
OPHELia, got it?

I AM WOMAN

By: Belinda Loya

I am woman, one with nature. The curves of my body are like the range of mountains, beautiful and imperfect.
My hair sways in the wind like the flow of the wheat and the barley in an open field.
My lips are salty like sand on a beautiful beach.
My strength is powerful like the waves crashing against one another.
My eyes are open and bright like the sun and moon at their highest.
My spirit is free, bobbing and weaving like a beautiful butterfly in a vast forest.
I am woman, one with nature.

We fight for movement and we fight for justice, but we also fight with one another.
We tear each other down and ridicule our imperfections, but we fail to see that when I look at you, I see myself.
What has been done to you, has been done to me. I know your hurt, I recognize it on the street.

I speak over it, trying to quiet the voice inside, but it has grown louder and louder.
Now THAT voice speaks because it has no choice.
It must come out, but what it says has no meaning.
The justice we once fought for has turned into an ocean of scrambled words that hurt, the hurt I see and recognize in the street.

You call me girly and sweet, but inside is a fire burning through that delicate flower you compare me to.
I struggle to obtain what you have, but I'll get there. My battle wounds show and I expect your respect but in return, you give me criticism.
I refuse to become irate and instead allow myself to receive this gift, this fluidity of strength that your oppression gives me.
Living a life without limits can be dangerous but I am not safe, I am not guarded, I am volatile and unpredictable.

SHE WAS ME

By: Juanita Chavez-Carrillo

I LOVE myself...
These curves that can
dance the night away
and the curly curls on
my head that have a life
of their own.
I LOVE myself...
SHE...she did not love
herself...
She did not like that
her tongue rolled so
much, that her clothes
smelled like tortillas,
and that her name was
too hard to pronounce
so she told her mom she
hated herself.
Pero mija! This is who
you are!
No, I told her.
I do not want to be this.
Pero que es this?
This is when I go to
school and am told
my name is weird and
if they can call me
something else because
Juana is too much work.
When I turn on the TV
and can't relate because
their portrayal of home
is not my home. They
have a white picket
fence, a mother named
Susan and a father
named Bill who works
for a law firm.

Law.
To not have to pretend
to respect the same
uniforms that can with
one decision decide to
separate me and you.
To have to sit next to
Chris and Austin in
class tell me that they
love their dads because
they protect us from the
bad guys, but what they
actually mean is protect
people like you from
people like us.
WE are the bad guys
mama!
I have to call home a
country that hates me.
That hates you.
Mama, I love you.
The strength of a
thousand warriors
wants to rip open from
my mouth, this tongue
of mine is a machete. I
yearn to cut through
the pain rip open these
scars and let them just
bleed.
I AM REAL.
I AM IMPORTANT.
I AM ANGRY.
I AM BEAUTIFUL.
I LOVE MYSELF.

MUCHA-CHONA

Cayó una hoja frágil al suelo
Levanto la mirada hacé arriba
Se sintió pequeña
Deseaba ser el árbol

Admiraba sus brazos fuertes, gordos
Contemplaba su tronco, firme
Libremente independiente...
Aguantaba los vientos que empujaban
Aguantaba la lluvia que limpiaba
Aguantaba sol, que quemaba
La hoja cayó frágil al suelo
Se sentía pequeña
Se sentía pequeña
Se sentía pequeña

Pero...
Permanecía a algo inmenso
Formaba parte de una estructura magnífica
Cayó una hoja frágil al suelo
Levanto la mirada hacé arriba
Admiro sus brazos, su tronco, su cuerpo
Fuerte
Gorda
Firme
Libremente independiente.

By: Estefania Garcia

CIELO

My mom called me "Cielo."
A name I didn't
understand but I never
questioned. See, it
directly translates to
sky, which was funny cuz
she always said I was her
world which was funny
cuz she was mine.
Mi Mama told me stories
of the women who came
before me and how they
held energies
ahead of their time,
mujeres poderosas, simply
divine.
See, it starts with my
great grandmother. She
could cook up a storm as
well as she could cook
up a meal. Who could both
start fights and finish
them.
Las doñas y señoras del
barrio talked about
her because they swore
resilient plus woman
must equal dangerous.
Because when a woman's
body was told to take up
more room than her voice,
She moved her caderas
back and forth to the
sound of Zambo Cavero,
waved her hand, and
screamed "no, there's room
for me."
Then the page turns
to illustrate my

grandmother, whose
prayers were as strong as
she.Each stanza said with
elegance, each word, each
plea.
Rosario in her hand and
Rocio on her hip, Abuela
held them close, holiness
molded both.
And she'd close her eyes,
for just a second take
a breath, look to the
heavens
saying
PACIENCIA Y FE, DOY
GRACIAS PORQUE
Diosito hizo al mujer en
su imagen y semejanza
Y eso si lo se.
Después came my
mother,who brought me
up with the knowledge
that I carry the lives of
the woman before us. That
we carry the lives of the
woman before us. Sazón
shakes off her hips, into
her stride, la negra
camina con orgullo, with
pride.With a love sweeter
than dulce de leche, she
held me,and blessed me,
and taught me, and raised
me up to know that mi
valor es un tesoro,
reminding me I come from
cocoa and stolen oro.
So when mi mama calls me
Cielo, I always smile.

By: Sofia Celeste

ESPÍRITU DE LEÓN

By: Karina Daza

Como un guerrero en el bosque,
Llevas el valor en tu sangre
Naciste a una familia que

Cría mujeres y hombres fuertes
Tu mamá vino a este país sin
nada,
Sin conocer más que tres
palabras
Con quinientos pesos en su
bolsillo
Ella se mató trabajando
Como la flecha que jalan hacia
atrás,
Ganas fuerza cuando te
arrastran
Con mucho poder vas a volar
Cuando tu superas, no lo
creerán
Deja que te lancen a los lobos
Saldrás liderando la manada
de ellos
Encajado en tu corazón

Vive el espíritu de león
Aunque nos llamen "Dreamers,"
Estamos despiertos.
Luchando.

Con ojos abiertos.

ALEGRIA PUBLISHING

MY HISTORY BOOKS ARE BETTER

By: Shireen Alihaji

than your history books
—because I wrote them.

"They never pick us,"
said the dandelion.
"That's why we grow
everywhere."

—wild flowers

MORE MELANIN IN MEDIA

By: Veronica Lopez

I am bored,
I am tired,
I am frustrated,
With the same
recycled faces and
storylines in media
That revolve around
whiteness,
That no longer
resonate, or have
never looked
anything like me.
We deserve better,
My fellow brothers
and sisters of color
and I deserve better
than this.
We deserve to see our
faces represented.
We deserve to see
ourselves at the
forefront of the
stories we love:
Whether it's coming
of age, falling
in love, going on
adventures,
Or dealing with the
struggles that our
culture brings,

We deserve to have
our stories told, old
and new,
Without a non-POC
being the epicenter,
or the savior.
We deserve
opportunities
without the
requirement
Of a few drops of
Caucasian DNA in our
blood,
Or of having to
be on the lighter
end of the melanin
spectrum,
So that we are more
tasteful and easy to
swallow.
We deserve
recognition without
the catch being that
It was just a quota
that needed to be
fulfilled
To serve a higher
purpose for greedy
needs.

THROUGH AN AGENT'S EYES

By: Ayling Zulema Dominguez

I saw you crying on the border. You stood on the U.S. citizen/passport-holding line, speaking to one of the migrants pitching camp on the asylum-seeking file. You looked at me con una mirada que mata . Growing up, my father had this saying — "Hay algunas mujeres que pueden, hasta solitas, tumbar gobiernos." Looking at you now, I hope he was right.

DIVINE INTERVENTION

By: Ayling Zulema Dominguez

Remember when tuvimos
que cambiar de pijamas
'cuz our shorts were too
short—they dared be what
their name intended—and
teníamos visita?
"But they're family!" I
protested. Origin story
of my nascent rebellion?
"No importa,
se ve mal..." Mami would
whisper back.
My mosquito bite tits
needed a training bra
, another layer of
clothing, one that no one
else but myself regularly
saw
whenever I dared sneak a
peek in the mirror,
a promiscuous act I would
normally steer clear of;
when Mami had already left
tempranito p'al trabajo
and Abuelita stood at
the stove warming up
hermanita's milk bottles.
Those were the only,
infinitesimal moments in
time where I could steal
prolonged looks at my
body.
That which, though
certainly no one made me
feel as such, was mine.
Another layer meant
to protect,

even though they were
already well-kept behind
the veil of secrecy and
mystery my family's
refusal to discuss them
had generated.
To guard, to protect... but
from what?
I could not for the life of
me comprehend why they
were so damn suspect.
From the monsters under
my bed?
Or, scarier yet, the ones
whose wrongdoing it is
to shame women for their
poder,
por simplemente ser.
Those that want you to
prepare your man's plate
before your own. That want
you home
before the street lights
come on
but don't blink twice
when Julián stays out late
because he's
the son.
The only thing that bra
was training me for
was divine intervention
to stop paying attention
to your machista ideals
'Cause anything you can do,
I can do better,
and all while wearing a
bomb-ass pair of heels.

WHISPERS

By: Vanessa Caraveo

Every turn I take, there
is a voice;
Other times, there is
more than one.
And in the darkest of
nights on those lonely
streets,
I can still be seen by
some who don't want me.
I am no creator but a
creation;
Different but the same
as the others.
They say it is not the
same
Because the difference
is clear in all I do.
I fight the urge to
suppress the ache I feel
Just because I want to
belong here:
A place where I am not
wanted

But a place I desire to
be and where I seek to be
accepted.
The days are longer
And I have nowhere else
to go.
Someday, I may be
welcomed,
Even by those who close
their hearts to me.
The whispers are sent to
taunt me,
Because I can tell what
it is about
But I will live like a
deaf human,
One who doesn't have to
endure cruel whispers.
Until then, I will walk
in pride of who I am
With the hope that
someday, we will live in
love and acceptance.

WHAT DOES IT MEAN TO BE A MUJER?

By: Alejandra Jimenez

I manifest divinity.
I am glorious and magical.
A galactic legacy.
I stride the earth's surface
with confidence as I am a
vigorous energy.
I am a Mujer!
One of conviction.
A transcending force
of progressiveness and
justice.
I manifest new life and
with it
the opportunity to correct
humanity's wrongs.
My fears are subsided
by my desire to see
equality prosper.
Oh, what a force to be
reckoned with!
I am a warrior of feminine
cunning
and will not be silenced.
A passion burning bright
fueled by
my lineage and sisterhood.
I am your mother, your
sister,
your wife, your daughter.
A full and sagacious
manifestation,
my voice delivers the
verity of my ancestors.
A reverberant existence
handed down from the wake
of feminine consciousness.
Seraph recipient,
I do not shy from my
psyche.
In my emotional depth you
will
find unassailable
strength.
You will not question my
authority,
not because you are
without right,
but because the
transparency of intention
to thrive
will leave no question in
your mind of my truth:
I am grounded and I am a
Mujer Grande!

AT ANY MOMENT

By: Alejandra Jimenez

Sometimes

When we are busy preparing
La birria para la cumpleañera
And the decorations for the
invitados

Sometimes

When we are all gathered together
Y escuchamos Cumbia y Norteña
O Cumbia-Norteña

When we have all finished eating
Y nos hemos cansado de platicar
We move all the tables and chairs
Para crear nuestra pista de baile

Sometimes

When we turn the music up
As loud as we want
y tía Violeta y tía Azucena
Begin to dance

When we laugh and laugh
Entre vuelta y vuelta
Bailando con los primos

Sometimes

When we hit the pinata
Cantando Dale, Dale, Dale
No pierdas el tino
Paraque todo el barrio nos oiga

When we sing "Las Mañanitas"
After "Happy Birthday"

Empezamos a corear que le
muerda, que le muerda
And smash the cumpleañera's face
Into the cake

Sometimes

When we feel so united
And safe
And free
Y feliiiiiiz

Sometimes

We forget
Though not truly
Que vivimos en una cárcel de oro
And when it is time to leave
Some of us must be extra
vigilant
Making sure not to raise
suspicions
of the patrolling cops
Porque no tenemos papeles

Sometimes

We forget that we live
With both feet planted here
But can be so easily uprooted

Sometimes

We forget the fear
That lives within us
Because we know
We know!
We could be torn apart
En———at
Cualquier———any
Momento————————moment.

PUZZLE PIECE

Looking back, I ignored it.

Steven.

Scanning the room
to fit the description
from the roaster, following the

Here!

through a maze of
colored children
in search of a pure soul

I sensed
disappointment
        in your tilt
        when the

Here!

led to me.

Did I have an extra ridge?
Unable to fit
        the bigger picture
of this puzzle,
        Steven?

No,
instead this piece was
Colored.

By: Steven Tovar

SOY COMO LAS OLAS

Soy como las olas,

Me digo a mí misma,

Parada frente a un mar bravo y
resonante
Mientras las veo ir y venir
infinitamente
Buscando un instante de permanencia.
Ni de aquí ni de allá.
Las olas cálidas y quietas del mar
Caribe

Donde mis pies de infante dieron sus
primeros pasos,
Son ahora olas frías y bravas

De un mar Pacífico

Donde mis pies adultos pisan
firmemente.
Ni de aquí ni de allá,

Pienso a mí misma mientras veo el
horizonte,
Recordando de donde vine

Y donde estoy.
Soy como las olas.

By: Romy Roloff

LLÁMENME MUJER

Dentro de todos los títulos
que tengo o los nombres que me
puedan llamar, llámenme mujer.
Mujer es fuerza y fragilidad.
Astucia y humildad.

Es caos y paz.

Mujer soy yo,
Y son mis hermanas.
Mujer es el amor que siento cada
mañana
Y la voz interna que me susurra
"sigue."
Mujer es vida y muerte.

Un pacto silencioso,
Una batalla eterna.
Mujer es el universo.
Y cuando escuche la llamada,
iré corriendo.

Por mí, por ella, por todas.

By: Romy Roloff

WORKING

By: Angela Valdez-Escobedo

Not eight but ten
Twelve hours a day.

The efforts of my king and
queen
Turned a suitcase
Into a life
In a strange country.

Even when carrying the
golden tickets that hold
fame
They were told they didn't
belong in the home of the
brave.
But the bravest thing I've
seen
Is them willingly giving
themselves
Aching bones, backs, and
bodies
For me to have a better
life.

They share stories
but to me they sound more
like nightmares.
Always having a survival
mentality.
Barely ever having
enough food on the table
For there were too many
mouths to feed.
Not being able to afford
basic necessities.

My father dropped out of
school in the third grade
In order to start working
And help his family.
While some mock my dad's
rough hands,
He will continue pulling
weeds
In order to buy me an
education.

My mother became the head
of the household
At nineteen
When her mother's life was
taken by a brain tumor.
Her first instinct wasn't
to lick her wounds
But to protect her
siblings
Because she feared
That the death of their
mother would be too much.

Growing up they taught
tight and distinct morals
Where we went to church
on Sundays;
Never take anything for
granted
because someone always
had it worse,
And remember to always
stay humble.

FROM THE TIME WE

begin to reason
life teaches us about
broken love
Busca tu otra mitad
(find your other half)
they say

only teaching us that
we are broken and not
whole
and desperately
we yearn for that
missing piece

as an adult now,
I questioned it,
I now know I am whole

I know my value as an
individual
and I am in no need of

mi otra mitad

soy única
soy fuerte
soy independiente

soy mi abuela
soy mi madre

soy cada ser humano
que he vivido
también soy mucho mi
padre

pero al final soy yo

I need you whole
not your half

soy tuya y soy de mi
sin nadie más.

By: Cynthia Villa

I AM A WOMAN

but I have never been a girl
I've always been a boy

I was born to win
I was born to lead

call me crazy
call me naïve
call me lesbian
call me feminist
call me anything you want

but don't call me weak
I belong with the pack

I am a woman
and I was born to lead.

By: Cynthia Villa

GENTRIFICATION

¿Abuela, dónde está la bodega?
Lo cerraron porque no podía pagar la renta.
Abuela, que és un Starbucks?
Una tienda de café lleno de azúcar y
precios ridículos.
Abuela, quien le dirá al Gringo que nuestro
café es negro y rico?
Ese es el problema, mi niña. El Gringo no
quiere saber de nada que es negro y rico
¿Abuela, entonces porque se mudan
a nuestro barrio?
Ay, mi niña, hace mucho que este barrio no es
ni nuestro, ni negro, ni rico.

By: Chiantelle Fernandez

MUJER LINDA

Me dicen mujer linda
mujer linda cuando
sonrió
mujer linda cuando
meneo mi cuerpo
mujer linda cuando
limpio y cocino
Pero cuando hablo
mi verdad con plena
actitud me dicen
ahí viene la odiosa
feminista.

By: Chiantelle Fernandez

I SEE YOU

By: Caroline Buendia

I see you, eyeing me
I've just entered but
I've got your undivided
attention
You crane your neck,
tall to my small frame
Your feet stomp the
direct line leading
to me
It's impossible not to
feel when your shadow
steps over mine
Your eyes loom down on
me like the cameras on
your walls
You've marked me a thief
without knowing who
I am
The caramel of my skin
has become the mud
under your shoes
The simplicity of me is
not enough
You ask me if I need
help in a tone that
reiterates you're
watching me

Expecting me to show
the truth behind my
color, at least the
truth you've given me
My whole being has
succumbed to that of
a person who does not
belong
My hands hide around
the pits of my arms to
assure you
My head bends below
your gaze
It's a shame how much
you make me feel
ashamed
As if I were the problem
As if I were everything
you make me to be
I hate myself for having
to prove myself, as I
prove
I am not the scum you
want me to be
I am not the problem
And just as you watch me
I see you too.

HE COULD HAVE BEEN

By: Caroline Buendia

I saw the corpse today
A man with the marked
skin that could never
fade
Painting the cement
with red
Dying for his unknown
sins
Dying for all he could
have been

Another black body on
the ground
Taking blame for
imagined possibilities
A thief, a criminal, a
thug
He could have been
Not just a man
Though a man is
all he was

And will no longer be

Unsolicited fear
Brought on by a hateful
past
A world where the dark
skinned weren't human
Nor were they treated
as such
Chained and mistreated
Fathers, sons, and
brothers
One after the other like
cattle
A chalked up sketch
Is what he's become
For all the horrible,
racist, and
stereotypical thoughts
Now he's just another
"He could have been..."

LIFE IS HARD MAMÁ

By: Mayra Montoya

and she said I know...

I've lived a dark winter

carried you through the storm

and birthed you from my bones.

Blood caught between my nails

in the hot burning stove

fragments of my kidneys

is the safe place you call home.

I WROTE MY NAME DOWN AND HE ERASED IT

By: Mayra Montoya

I swam in the water and he pulled me back to shore

I gave him all I had and he said, "give me more"

He asked me to speak and then silenced me

In hush tones and frightening stares

He took all I had but no one cared.

FROM EL NORTE

By: Teresa Castillo

When the sun comes up in the morning,
with rays that stretch out to touch the dew on the leaves,
They tuck away within the mounds of dirt,
perfectly lined across great plains.
The fog is dense and creeps above the agriculture.
The fresas, cilantro, lechugas and repollo.
The fog is dense and creeps above the people.
They tuck away,
to shy away from the cold in the early morning,
from the sun in the afternoon.
They wake before their children, to look after themselves,
for the sole purpose of bringing el pan a la mesa.
They come home tired, still looking to change the world they live in,
through ambition, tough work, and mounds of hope in education.
My grandfather crossed the border, through false identification. My twin aunts followed, at the early age of sixteen.
They packed away their clothes onto school-designed backpacks and alongside well-paid coyotes, crossed the vast desert through the night.
They slept in the corner of a dining room;
sacrificed to send money to their siblings.
In Mexico, my mother among them,
young and unafraid, for my aunts hushed their real experiences with gifts sent
from el norte.
They were so ignorant as to periods and feminine hygiene products. They put on a maxi pad, upside down, adhesive side up,

and became red with pain on
the perfectly lined mounds
of dirt.
Sacrifice.
They took it upon
themselves to live in a
world of English where
Español was only present
in the
dark creases of the
neighborhoods
they passed, over the years.
They had only themselves,
trapped between two worlds,
no bridge for connection.
Their father, the protector,
who brought them here to
work. Was he the definition
of a true feminist?
For the sake of keeping his
family alive and well,
treated his oldest
daughters as equals to
his sons.

Send them to work, not find
a husband.
For he...
He was off in late night
cantinas while they slept
beside each other on that
cold hard floor.
Ignorance is bliss,
but education is praised.
If you allow it,
it creeps alongside the fog
that rises in the morning,
and the sun rays dry it up.
The fresas, cilantro,
lechugas, and repollos come

As gifts from el norte.

They no longer come
hushed or enveloped in
deep secrets. They come
as stories grown from
experience. From el norte to
the north.

PROMESA VIVA!

By: Mónica Amelia García

Soy la suma de mis
antepasados, semilla de
sangre indígena!
Mi corazón esta tejido a
mi piel morena!
Bailo con la brisa y
fluyo con el rio!
Soy propósito andante,
aunque los extranjeros
me llamen inmigrante!

Somos las estrellas
ocultas en los libros de
historia!
Cristobal nunca nos
robó la victoria!
Tierras robadas llevan
nuestra huella!
Cada granito de la
tierra conoce nuestro
cantar!
Nuestras manos nunca
dejaron de trabajar!
Soy el fruto de batallas
heróicas!

Soy la oración de mis
ancestros y la semilla
de sus tierras mágicas!

Yo no nací para
cosechar el sueño
Americano!
Ese sueño no lleva la
bandera de mi paisano!
Fronteras no van a
limitar mis sueños!
Mis sueños llevan mil
rostros!

No soy semilla de
mortales!

Soy amanecer que
cultiva fuerza de lo
imposible!

Soy semilla de una
promesa viva!!

CHAMPIONS!

I evolved from the crumbs of broken
hearts, from a line of women whose
voices were silently ROARING!
Broken stairs made to hinder their
rise, their identity made invisible,
obscured by the mouth of greed.
Dreams hung on trees, spirits
slowly fading within, warriors
hiding in their own skin.
My worth became a slow reveal,
flight held captive by the systems
of gender oppression. For years,
I baptized myself with tears of
RESISTANCE!!
My eyes were given narrow pathways
but my heart swallowed the truths
whole, denying my expected docile
role.
I do not have to remind you that I
grew in the dark. My resilience is
historical, behold the RADIANCE!
My womb did not just carry babies,
it was a temporary residence where
guerreras were made! My body
contains scars amongst fields of
skin I will never trade.
You will see many of my kind
unsilenced and untamed: my sisters
channeling their warrior mothers
and grandmothers, occupying and
sharing space, our powers are
REVOLUTIONARY!
We are the mujeres with backbones
that don't bend; champions whose
dreams have no foreseen end.

By: Mónica Amelia García

SILENCE

How long do I have to stay quiet,
in order to not offend you?
How long do I have to stifle my soul,
before it runs out of air to breathe?
The pain I endure in silence
because you cannot bear to hear it out loud.

Cannot bear to hear my greatness.
To you, it means
there's less to go around.

To defy you is disrespect
So I must take your insults and
Wear them like a crown.

Wear them defiantly
because if I speak,
it is not only my soul you will try to break,
but my bones too.

By: Maria Padilla

REVEL

Take a look in the mirror and
revel in your beauty.
Revel in the woman you are.
Revel in your freckles
in your acne,
in your scars.
Revel in your stretch marks,
your rolls
your heart.
Revel in the beauty that you are.

By: Maria Padilla

LICENSE FOR EXPOSURE

By: Andrea Ramos

give them the license
to be the main stars not
side chicks,
supporting the
supporting stars, the
dark skinned latinos
aren't light enough,
the darker skinned
blacks aren't
aesthetic enough
they're not godly
enough,
even though I heard
before that god made
them first

left them in the earth
to grow their roots and
they reached all over
they are the ones not
allowed the roles
except as
maids and gardeners and
gangsters and prisoners

the ones with broken
english or no english
and five minute
screen time
or the loyal doorman or
cook in a run down shop

jokes are made on their
thick tongue
but learning two
languages is more than
i can even do right now
but no stories on why or
how they got there and
that others are
successful in
the country

instead of giving the
curvy, big ass, and
light skinned latinas
and black girls the
main roles,
give the indigenous,
the afro latinas,
the ebony skinned
black girls
the spotlight to show
you that we
are a part of the
culture too and
it's not all spicy mamis.

we are more than sex
symbols, maids,
and gangsters
we are so much more.

LIMITLESS

By: Heidy Marie

Soaring through the
skies without doubts
The ability to reach
heights never sought
With the resilience to
never stay down
The strength to destroy
whatever comes my way
Being Limitless

Renewed and no longer
askew
Shining brightly in
obscurity
Conquering everything
within gander
Pulverizing boulders
in my path
Being Limitless

Unattainable I stand
Master of my
circumstances
Standing without
remorse or regret

Never ashamed of any
transgressions along
the way
Being Limitless

Powerful and strong
Never shying away from
the challenges I face
A voice of reason, A
voice of truth
Never deaf, never mute,
never blind to see your
truth
Being Limitless

Humbly rising before
all
Proud of who I've become
Never wavering on my
convictions
With the predilection
of acceptance
Being unsurpassable
Being Limitless.

THE FORGOTTEN

By: Rocio Garcia

We continue to resist
the topic,
Not fully advocating
for them.
Shunning even our
loved ones
During family
gatherings.

We minimize their
existence
Due to ignorance
of what they are
experiencing.
Labeling, mocking and
dehumanizing them
Becomes second nature.

As we allow society
To grab a firm grip on
them,
Relief settles in,
And we convince
ourselves they are safe
now.

Behind bars they may
finally
Receive treatment.

Behind bars they may
finally
Get their needs met.

But behind bars,
They are again deprived
of their dignity.
Only to be labeled
Criminal.

Prison has become the
new warehouse,
Where we allow the
mentally ill to be
housed.
Where we allow our most
vulnerable population,
To be stored in cell
blocks and be forgotten.

Neglecting how
everything could have
been prevented,
Washes our hands from
guilt.
Allowing us to forget
Our role in social
change.

WAS IT WORTH IT?

By: Davina Ferreira

If you ask me
If it was worth the pain,
Not seeing my parent's age,
Living abroad,
to embark out on my own,
Build empires of hope
in a place so unknown,
I would tell you:

  -I don't quite know, most
days I am glad/ I have
flown over the weight/ of
my own limited/ outlook
of the world /where I had
grown, but others, I do
wonder-

If you are an immigrant.
If you once abandoned
everything and everyone
you loved,
Then you know.

Was it worth it?
The new house and monthly
mortgage?
The dream of "freedom" as
stardom?
The chasing and the
getting?
The accolades and the
sound of nearby fortune?

You tell me.
Mi Hermano,
Mi hermana
Emigrante.

Was it worth the pain,
The bleeding profits,
The nights of terror and
consolation?
The testing of your own
self - will and power?

  -if you ask me, I can tell
you. A good thing is / I
learned to fly beyond my
limits/ saw deadly fear
and crushed it with my
own fingers/ exchanged my
certainty for limitless/
became a delusional
dreamer, learned the value
of a day's work, prayed in
gratitude, humbled-

You tell me.
Mi Hermano,
Mi hermana
Emigrante.

LAVANDERÍA

By: Alexis Jaimes

There she is
pulling clothes out
and pushing piles into
machines
with the help of little
brother
or maybe son
or maybe cousin
or maybe kind stranger

here, we are all familia

She is a chemist, a
doctor, a witch in one
generation and a mother
of god in the previous
She is an apothecary, an
apprentice because she
still needs help from an
elder— guidance

She feeds purple, green,
blue potions into metal
cubes turning dirty
laundry to this week's
clothing

Man in a blue hat carries
around an empty mayo jar
rattling with coins and
crumpled dollars
His sign reads
Jesus se murió el pasado
domingo
Today we celebrate by
cleaning
los domingos are about
washing away last week's
sins
At least that's what it
was when I used to go to
church
It remains for others
though

The blue hat was bobbing
around in a quiet voice
and loud gestures
slapping two palms
together and slicing the
air with a display of
appreciation

No one truly knows if
it's a scam
Jesus might be real
or the photo of him on
the jar was downloaded
from Google
with the watermarks and
borders intact

or it could be true
because so many die
young around these parts
What's one more? they
say—
one too many

The magic woman pulls
and pushes burdens into
the drying machine
the 50-cent one because
it fits all the clothes

The other elders train
the younger ones
They continue the
tradition and teach—as
other generations have—
that this struggle is
necessary and they say:
this pain will make you a
kinder person
because then you will
understand what it means
to work hard
and others will make fun
of you for that
and that will make you
hurt
and that hurt—that
metallic taste you feel in
your chest—is what will
make you a kinder person
don't let the mercy be
burnt out of you
like a candle at church
because we are all magic
and we know how to make
potions and use them to
turn dirt into clean.

HISTORICAN

By: Joseph Vazquez

"Land of the great
lords,"
or the great land called
Borinquen.
Home of the peaceful
Taino, Arawak Indians.
Lived there since about
500 B.C.
until the Spanish
Europeans came and
conquered
while bringing their
diseases to kill off
those peaceful Tainos.

The Spaniards forced
them in to slavery,
raped the women, then
married them
and somewhere in there
they got African slaves
in to the mix or in to
the pot
and after years of being
stirred, a Puerto Rican
is what they got.
They tried to kill off
our culture and their
diseases played the role
as vultures,
but in the 1800's we took
the role as soldiers
and started up-rises
and started bumrushing
those Spaniards like
bulldozers.

Then came the Americans
acting like they felt

we were worth less than
spit, but in reality, to
them, we were just some
dirty spics
who were perfect for the
role of hard laborers
and they knew we weren't
troublemakers
so they thought they
could abuse our
abilities while
they earned all the
paper.

They put us into poverty
while they used us to
boost their economy
then forced us to commit
cultural blasphemy
so we started
contemplating on
measures that were
going to have to be taken
drastically.

They were mistaking our
kindness for weakness
until we decided to do
something about the
mistreatment they tried
to keep as a secret.
Pa'lante! Siempre!
Pa'lante! was in the
hearts of the Young
Lords in the late 60's
as they revolted and
moved swiftly
much work was needed
cause change never
comes quickly.

From Chicago to the
South Bronx, these young
rebels fought against
many devils raising the
standards to a new level
in the ghettos where we
settled.

But then came more
problems later on in time
where they sent us to
Vietnam to fight on the
front lines
while back at home they
provided heroin, Brown
Rhine
like how they provided
the Native Americans with
the "inner city" wines
to have people like us
perform our own genocide.

They tried to keep us
blind, but in the late
70's early 80's Blacks and
Latinos found refuge in
break dancin' and spittin'
rhymes.
They dropped the line, we
kicked the beat
by bringing that Bomba
rhythm to the streets,
but then America
introduced us to crack
as they kept their
persistence to keep us off
our feet.

After getting rid of
the Young Lords they
perceived us as ruthless
and reckless while

America had their military
in our land doing bomb
tests in Vieques.
They claimed that right
and when it comes to war
Puerto Rico can fight,
but when it comes to the
Presidential election,
Puerto Rico can't
participate
yet America still strives
to make our land the fifty-
first state,
but when our communities
are in their worst state
they don't even regard us
in their political debates.

We have what we have now
because we took it into our
own hands
our own fate.
We have one of the biggest
parades of the year because
of the sacrifices and
bloodshed we suffered in
that war against hate
in that war against those
who discriminate.
There's no more military
in Vieques because a once
sleeping lion is now awake
you trespass in his jungle
and his anger you will
taste.
That lion that has
awakened lies in the heart
of every Puerto Rican
a lion that will make sure
everyone hears us when
that lion is speaking.

CONVERSATIONS WITH THE MAINTENANCE WORKER

By: Monica Mendoza

The maintenance worker comes in to fix our kitchen sink's drainage. I stand next to him as I prepare my basic lunch of spaghetti. He looks at my curls and asks where I'm from. "Soy Mexicana. De Guerrero." He replies, "Costeña."

He asks me how classes are going. He goes into story mode and starts talking to me about how intelligent his son is. He was Columbia bound. Invested $12,000 on his son's room and board in New York. He backed out at the end for love. Stayed in California for some amazing girl that studies Chicano Studies. He tells me, "She's so smart. She's at Berkeley now. She's like the daughter I never had." I smile at the thought of this intelligent woman that he wanted to claim as his blood. He says, "I'm still paying off the $12,000."

His second son was a social worker. He wanted to help people. Did it

for three years and got tired. He gave up to pursue his dream of being a musician. He lives in limbo now. In instability, but he's somehow pushing forward.

He says his sons have curly hair like mine. Their mother is Guatemalan and Jamaican. She's a Mulatta. He tells me I sort of look like her. He's an organizer. He informs other Guatemalans about their rights here. He studied political science before coming to the United States. He now manages an apartment complex in Los Angeles. Fixes the drainages, the lights, the plumbing, he keeps the whole building moving.

"I love my family. As much as they're a mess, I love them and their dreams."

He leaves once the drainage is fixed. I leave five minutes later, suddenly yearning to hear my immigrant parent's voices.

SUEÑOS

By: Monica Mendoza

I have dreamt of
what this reunion
would look like
My life revolving
around the thought
of my undocumented
parents
The day my father
will hug his mother
again
27 years later, 1
marriage later,
2 kids later, one
death later
2,500 miles later,
one phone line
two flights, one visa

How many steps will
it take them to reach
each other?
To extend an arm and
wrap it around each
other
Fingerprints, sweat,
and tears, all in one
place
Will we feel
fulfilled again?
Mother and children
reunited once again

The angels will
dance with joy above
us
La Virgen with her
arms stretched
around us
A godly moment
A prayer in fruition

An embrace that only
took
27 years, 1 marriage
later, 2 kids later,
one death later
2,500 miles later,
one phone line
two flights, one visa
We are still
dreaming.

WHITE LINES

White lines

Squares

Rectangles

Corners

Though riddled with
Clorox and Fabuloso
asthma and allergies

Mami stayed knees to
the ground

Poison in pincer
grasp

etching out white
lines
small but heavy hands
White lines
All
Hector Lavoe y Marvin
Gaye
White lines
White lines

All raid and roach
motels

All moth balls and
stray cats turned pets
to keep our clothes
from being eaten by

famished mice

Leggings and T-shirt

Large belt at the waist

All Whitney Houston y
La India

All Motown and salsa

All salsa y hustle

All high heels and hip
swish

All lipstick and code
switch

All dollar cabs and
tokens

All conductors cars
and elevator doors
open

To skyscraping
cubicles

Mami stayed

All

Coffee and dry clean
gettin'

All white capitalist
voice and vernacular
phone answerin'

All wealthy white men
and women

By: Kimberly Rosario

yelling in her face
White lines

Chalking out the
crevices where she knew
roaches had been
White lines

Before laying out the
bait

White lines

Before opening windows
and potpourri

White lines

But still

Brown wings

The spiked leg

Or entire roach corpse

Surfacing among our no
frills corn flakes

The crunch of the body
shocking

Overpowering the soggy
flavorless discs

Igniting disgust

Triggering gag reflex

But vomiting suppressed
because often we were
famished too

and at least we got to eat
half the bowl
White lines
The feel of cold concrete
just beneath the skimpy
layer
White lines

And white chalk before
tootsie roll brown
plastic moldings

Against flat,
seamless, amber speckled
tile

White chalk drawn
around the perimeter of
a home

In her best effort to
keep everything within
it safe.

ALEGRIA PUBLISHING

TREE IN SIDEWALK SQUARE

Like the tree that grows in an urban
sidewalk
They try to contain our roots

Nuestras raíces

Under the heavy cement of the sidewalk
square
But they enjoy our trunk our branches and
leaves
Our beauty

Our music, our nutrition

Our language every now and then
But our roots are in the basin of the
square

Our ancestors, our past, our blackness,
our indigenous people
Nuestros países

Underneath the heavy cement of the
sidewalk square
Our roots feel heavy

We try to escape

The cement cracks as we grow
We regain control.

By: Veronica Polanco

YOU SHOULD
BE AWARE

By: Clare Miranda

I walked into a funeral;

One of those funerals of
a family member.
I didn't know this
family member

but everyone else
around me did.

They said nice things
about this Tia of mine,
a great, great-aunt.

I didn't know this
family member,
but my mother certainly
did.

Some family members
who knew her better
Spoke about her.
One at a time,
these people

With their beautiful
brown faces

Sauntered their way up
to the microphone

Each eager to say what
they remembered of her
the most.

"Oh, she loved her

family," they said.

The other brown faces
nodded in agreement
"Oh, she loved her
family and children,"
they said.
The nods continued.
"Oh, she loved her
family and kept an
immaculate house."

"Oh, and her cooking was
amazing, everyone loved
her food. Didn't you all
enjoy her food and when
she would serve you?"
Yes, the brown faces
said.
"Oh, her tamales were
the best. Always the
perfect flavor and
consistency. Weren't
her tamales the best?
How she would spend all
day to make the perfect
tamales for everyone?"
"Oh yes, Tia, was the
best at cooking."
Her food was the best.
Her recipes were the
best.
Her house was the
cleanest and the best."
I thought her funeral
would be a place where

I could learn more
about her.
Instead, I just learned
that she kept a clean
house, she took care
of people
and her tamales were
the best.
These things are
important, yes they are.
The people who do these
things for their family
should be admired and
honored and shown
gratitude.
Was Tia ever asked if
this is what she wanted
to do?

What did she like to eat?
What TV shows did she
enjoy watching?
Was she fiery and
outspoken or quiet and
peaceful?

Did she dress up ever
or did she prefer to be
simple and plain?
Was she happy?
Was she fulfilled?
These things I never
knew for they were never
said by any of the people
who spoke of her
, the people who had
taken from her what she
had freely given over the
years:

Her time,

Her energy,

Her love.
People talk of
colonizers:

How people from Europe
came and took what they
wanted and needed
From the indigenous
people who didn't
know better

Or weren't able to stand
up for themselves.
The biggest threat
today

Are the colonizers in
your own family
Or your own friends

Or your loved ones.
The ones who will take
from you what you give
And then take some more.
Who eat and then
gotta run.

The ones who will tell
you that they wish they
could stay longer, that
the next time the visit
will be longer, it just
didn't work out today
but we will plan again
soon and then give you a
brief kiss on the cheek.
Beware of the
colonizers in your
own family

Amongst your
own friends

Amongst those closest
to you
The ones who will
spend their whole
life around you
Taking what they
need from you without
gratitude
Only to thank you and
only to remember you
When you are in a box

On display

And are surrounded
By brown faces.
Colonizers can come
in any color.
And it's the ones
closest to you
The ones that look
like you

They will be the ones
Who take the most
from you.

MY LIBERATION

I walk on broken
roads
Tipping and toeing
around rubble and
rocks.

I breathe in toxins
precipitated by
forces of corruption.
Forces of all-too-
familiar paradoxes.

The scene is fiery
from unresolved
tension
And I suffocate.

For long before my
time, there was a
preordained creed
That diminished my
essence to a vessel.

A basin made
to dilute the
perversion of the
male gaze
And I shrink.

With every vile
stare, I shiver with
disgust.
And I shrink.

Generations
of mandatory
performances have
worn on me.
And I weep.

Praise only for my
self-sacrifice at the
expense of my sanity.
And I weep.

God knows I have
pained through the
sprouting of my seeds.
And my seeds now echo
my flesh.
Enigma no more.
A permutation of
dignified depths is
imperative
To the rebirth of my
soul.

Only now, I stand
unbolted with the
unearthing truth
That my cry is my
salvation.

And only I can set
myself free.

By: Diana R. Diaz

70

LAS VIOLETAS

By: Paloma Alcantar

Llueven lágrimas
amargas de ellas,
sí, de esas que hoy ya no
están,
de mujeres silenciadas
con sólo una mirada,
de aquellas que soñando
con ser princesas,
terminaron prisioneras
en la celda del castillo.
De palomas mensajeras
que nunca arribaron.

Lentamente van los
cielos elevándose,
ante la oquedad de sus
trémulos pasos,
atravesando el umbral
de las quimeras.
Desde el Norte hasta Sur
y del Este al Oeste,
igual que las violetas
en primavera,
van por allí danzando
con el cabello
alborotado.

¡Ah! Pusilánime mundo el
nuestro,
que no las acoge entre
sus brazos.
Altivas almas de
valientes guerreras.
Torbellinos de un amor
desparpajado.
Buscándose van entre
las promesas rotas,
que les vendieron al
pasar de los años.

El sexo débil sin piedad
les llamarón,
y nadie les contó que era
un abrupto engaño.
Alaban a las de su linaje
que la voz desafiaron,
y desde sus trincheras
reclaman un trato
igualitario.
Mas las heridas del
pasado no han sanado,
ni la eternidad que les
tatuaron en los labios.

Libres, feministas,
locas, brujas, nazis,
de tantas formas las han
llamado.
Frente a un pueblo
repleto de cobardes,
que en un santiamén las
sigue juzgando.
Sublime melancolía
ocultan las estrellas,
menospreciando la
utopía que tejen sus
manos.

Inocentes sonrisas que
de noche tiemblan,
al abrigo de un amor
inconsumado.
Alas teñidas de liberta
sueñan ellas,
para las flores
soberbias que no han
llegado.
Gritos de auxilio a una
justicia ciega y
mujeres que a susurros
lo siguen intentando.

COULDN'T KEEP IT LOCKED AWAY (ESCÚCHAME)

By: Scarllet Veras

centuries worth of
silences, weap-heavy
trauma from
being disowned / displaced
from our countries, our
homelands: choked, gripped
by the throat burnt /
stuffed
nails leaving luna-sized
imprints on bruised skin

my longings have been
hidden within my ribcage
& as I
hungered for the sea to
hold me amongst its waves
I took
a blade upon the wrist
as though its dragging
embrace would
gift me a semblance of
control

(juventud perdida a la luz
oscura, a las tumbas del
cementerio, a espejos
irregulares, a terreno
muerto / mi
cabello oscuro se cayó en
pedazos y yo sólo miraba,

mis ojos
dolor inyectados en
sangre vidriosos)

what I mean to say
is that no sé cómo
comenzar, tengo el
mundo, mis antepasados,
mi familia dominicana
en mi garganta
el agua nunca ayuda a mi
sed, la tos resistida en
silencio, esa
sombra sobre mí siempre
asesina mi mente

nights spent pressing
my arms around my soft
middle, la ciudad
viviendo como si nada
estuviera mal entre los
silencios, the
deepest parts of me
aching to fade away &
float among our
suppressed / unspoken
history

lo que quiero decir es
cómo me duele el alma,

quieren
nuestras historias,
nuestra sangre, nuestras
lágrimas —
wringing them from our
veins & our pores & our
thick hair
& strong core & our lives
and becoming drenched by
them

nos quedamos callados
por las mismas manos de
nuestra familia
sosteniendo, nuestrxs
palabras atrapadas,
nuestrxs hijxs,
nuestrxs niñxs lastimadxs
y encerradxs, la puerta un
escudo
más fuerte que el acero
(pero no más)

interpretan el silencio
como acostarse a dormir /
siendo cómplices
en la apropiación de
nuestra cultura. (no es
verdad) es más como fuego
ardiendo en los ojos, humo

saliendo de los oídos. mi
psicóloga me
ha dado el espacio para
desenredar todo lo que
nunca hemos discutido

encontré mi esperanza,
brillo como los rayos del
sol en los
días de verano en NYC, los
niñxs jugando en la bomba de
agua, el aire tierno. nada
duele & everything is tinted
in gold
hoop earrings, mango juices
dripping down mosquito
bitten arms

skin is tender & sticky
after spending the whole day
outside, never
looked more alive. dewy
grass tickling bare toes /
fingertips raised up,
reaching past the passed
down silences, grasping a
lifeline of resistencia
& spilling out iridescent
triumph to revive our
weathered bodies.

RESIST

By: Alessandra Felicia Rea

We close our eyes and try to dream,

But the past is our nightmare.

In the night, you stole us from our native land.

During the day, you robbed us of our dignity.

You took our resources and broke the tender heart that was inside us.
So, we resisted.
We used to roam the land with a freedom only the birds of the sky could reach,

But you captured us calling us savages while taking our children.

The identity that was woven into the most sacred part of our

being you tried to mutilate,
But you failed.
You only left wounds, but oh how they bleed centuries on.

So, we continue to resist.
Because of the way we speak, the way we look, the way we pride ourselves,
you mock us and try to humiliate us.

You spit lies, slurs, and hate because you're afraid of us.

You try to civilize, oppress, threaten, and annihilate us;
But guess what, you can't triumph over us.
Because we resist.
We unite, but all you do is criticize us.

Do you enjoy your silly attempts to feel superior?

Do you find contentment
in the suffering your
selfishness imposed on
all of us?
Well, the only fruit you
can speak for is the sin
we call your ego.

For your only legacy
is the generations
of idiocracy and
hypocrisy.

Because you resist.
Generations have
passed, and history
repeats itself.

Our stories, our hope,
our will becomes
stronger.

A fire ignites from deep
inside us, it unites us.

And soon you won't be
able to continue to
fight us.

Because we will never
cease to resist in
hope that one day, you
welcome us.

MAY DAY

By: Alexis Ybarra

Once clear water fell from the sky
Now darkness flows down the
highways into the pipe lines.
Into the ocean where the trash
is now stored.
Floating with the fishes.
Off it goes.

Floods trapping children in homes,
Roads blocked.
Homes destroyed.
We still continue to turn a blind eye
into the void.

Yellow water in Flint.
Puerto Rican lives unchecked.
Nicaraguan people murdered.
Where can the people go?

The Moon won't save us, Mars
is years away?
How do we save us from ourselves?
May Day.

WHAT HAPPENED TO JUSTICE?

I would speak for you.
"It's real! Justice exists!"
It did.
I no longer speak for you.

In turn, you placed
Mis Hermanos
Mis Hermanas
In cages
In the land of the free.

Mis Hermanos
Mis Hermanas
You risk your wings
To land in a net of safety.
Now that same net entraps you.

Day in, day out.
If the days ever end.
They discuss your release.
Surface level words
Come from surface level
Knowledge.

A mighty power
Given to so few.
Majority tyranny.
It exists in the Republic.

By: Sharon Ayala

MANGO DREAM

By: Wendy Garcia

Mango dream,

Ruby lips,

Wavy hair,

Swaying hips,

Sharp tongue,

A mind of your own,

But always afraid,

Of being alone.

Your men indulged,
Heavy handed,

Scarred their livers,

Left you stranded,

With children to raise,

Decisions to make,

Cockroaches to chase,

A heart that breaks.

Your hand grew heavy,

Just like your men,

Blessed art thou among women,
Pray for us sinners,
Amen.
One by one,

Your children leave,

Or they die,

All but me.

Years go by,

And you chop away,

Wall by wall,

Night and day,

Mr. Time waits for no one,
Your last breath awaits,

You beg me to help you,
From those pearly gates.
Despite it all,

I aim to please,

To keep you on earth,
Chasing your mango dream.

FUERTE

By: Cindy Monterrosa

Fuerte.
Grounded.
En los hombros de mi mami.
She carries me always.
Volando alto, sin miedo. Respiro fuerte.
Exhalo.
Recuerdo donde estoy.
Being carried by mi mami.
Mujer sabia.
Manos cansadas.
Hombros agachados.
El mundo venciéndola.
Nunca.
Ven mami.
Te cargo yo.
En mis hombros.
I will carry you always.
Mujer sabia.
Con manos cansadas.
Corazón grande.
Repira fuerte mami.
Exhala.

FEET MOVING ALONG TO GET THERE

By: Blanca Figueroa

I walk slowly, and then hurriedly without
a place to go but I'll get there
I am looking down to ensure I am still
moving
I keep going because I have to get there
I don't know yet, but it's better than back
there is what I hear
I somehow trust and keep my feet moving
I only know to move without thinking of
plans
I will get there because that is why I'm
still moving my feet
I am accompanied by generations to come,
and mostly those generations I will not
meet
All of this I didn't know when I started
moving my feet.

NIÑA BUENA

La boca cerrada
y bien pintada
Los codos no van sobre la mesa
cada cubierto para cada cosa
Que te abran la puerta
que te paguen la cuenta
Escucha atenta
hazlo sentir importante
Sonríe
Ríete pero no tan fuerte
Sino nadie te va a escoger
tienes que ser niña buena
Niña buena
Niña buena
Niña buena
Pero no mujer
La mujer es prohibida
ella siente y ama
piensa y habla
tiene voz
es una luz encendida
es la dadora de vida
Eso es un peligro
para el hombre
y para el mundo
Mantente callada
tu a lo tuyo
a la casa
a verte linda
como de revista
Preocúpate por encontrar pareja
ese hombre que te proteja
a ti niña buena.

By: Roberta Bárcena

COMPLICATED

By: Astrid Ferguson

A compiled Licorice
People with tasteless
buds
Left behind in corner
stores.

En mi barrio
We call them bodegas.

The places where
neighboring cats
rest
Tethering souls
converse
Over Yucca's and
Platanos
Banderas hang over
doorways
Trumpets sing
through woofers and
beat-up speakers.

The same place where
Doritos and Onion
Rings
Can be both fried,
Lays, or bagless.

It's a place where
Hispanic
Caribbean
Mis Hermanos can
own.

Own their tongues,
High pitches
And stories.

Even if sometimes
they forget to pay
their rent in a timely
fashion.

A location where sodas
like
Frambuesa and Pepsi
Can shimmy in the same
nevera.

Yet, in this same place
The Spanglish is not
considered creative
enough
To cure trauma or
Intellectual enough to
question supernatural
theories.
Consistently declined
by the men in blue vest
and heavy artillery.
Revoked by those who
carry suitcases.
Renewing their
favorite colored
stamps;
Forgotten,
Insidious,

Disruptive,
Anything to shred
our applications
like flour.
One by one reducing
our names to
delinquents
returning home.

Tossing us out of
buildings
Without parachutes
Gambling whose teeth
will splatter the
farthest.

As if continent lines
weren't thick enough.

When you asked our
neighborhood for our
zip codes we respond
as one block
Complicated
Complicated
Complicated

For we always
wondered
What it must be like
to play hopscotch
Without hiding every
time
A siren was heard.
Oh how it must be
To learn to play
Tablas,

Embrace carefree West
coast living,
And read silently
without nerves
yelling
LOOKOUT
A bullet penetrated a
window,
Thief and/or an
officer can be the same
Person forcing a new
way in.

Reporters questioning
witnesses
While all we can
muster is...
Complicated
Complicated
Complicated

Then a prized jewel
is found in my only
suitcase
The only book owned by
my abuela
A journal that reads,
Do you know why we
learned to balance
baskets full of fruits
on our heads?

Because it was the
only way
To keep our complex
madres safely rooted
on our heads.

WHO AM I?
QUIEN SOY?

A divine woman
Una mujer divina

A woman with strong
beliefs
Una mujer con fuertes
creencias

A compassionate woman
Una mujer compasiva

A loving woman
Una mujer amorosa

A woman full of
curiosity and wonder
Una mujer llena de
curiosidad y maravilla

A woman who champions
the way for herself and
other women
Una mujer que defiende
el camino para ella y
otras mujeres

A woman who finds the
positive in it all
Una mujer que
encuentra lo positivo
en todo

A woman who breaks the
mold
Una mujer que rompe el
molde

A woman who reveals
her soul
Una mujer que revela
su alma

A woman who is on a
mission to impact the
world
Una mujer que tiene la
misión de impactar al
mundo

A woman who makes her
own rules
Una mujer que hace sus
propias reglas

A woman who dances
to the beat of her own
tunes
Una mujer que baila al
ritmo de sus propias
canciones

A woman who pushes
through her fear
Una mujer que supera
su miedo

By: Susie Aguilar

A woman who leaps
through the unknown
Una mujer que salta
a través de lo
desconocido

A woman who paves
the way for future
generations to come
Una mujer que allana
el camino para las
futuras generaciones

A woman who extends
a hand to those
wanting to make a
change
Una mujer que
extiende una mano a
quienes desean hacer
un cambio

A woman who embraces
her roots
Una mujer que abraza
sus raíces

A woman who is proud
of her uniqueness
Una mujer orgullosa de
su singularidad

An unorthodox woman
is who I AM
Una mujer poco
ortodoxa es quien SOY

Now, the question is,
do you know who you
are?
Ahora, la pregunta es,
¿sabes quién eres?

TO BE A MOTHER OR NOT TO BE

By: Davina Ferreira

To be a mother or
not to be,
that is the question,
I ask myself.

Some friends say
that giving birth is
to die and be reborn
again.

A new woman is born,
the old one gets
shredded,
Gone as her old loves
archived under her
broken bones.

Scars all around,
Stiches up and down,
Her sacred body
stretched out,
Nipples tortured.

Then,
You see your baby's
face and you realize
someone just became

your very life
And perhaps your own
death.
You have never loved
ANYONE that way!

To be a mother or not
to be...
One must die to taste
the sweetest of all
loves.

– "The greatest of them
all.'
–They say.

A deeper love than I
have never felt before.

But to die again?

Am I willing to agonize
once more for that one
great love?

I'm tired of dying now.

I'm finally living.

Now that I am finally
walking on my own
womanly sky,
creating my victory
with prideful
strides,
a muse to myself
at last.

Finally accepting
of my gifts and my
curves,

fully and
unapologetically a

WOMAN.

To be a mother or not
to be...

Sometimes I fantasize
when strollers pass
me close by,
I imagine his red
hair and light

grandmother's eyes, a
dreamy smile,
I seem to grasp from
another lifetime.

But a bit too quickly,
I go back to my
Daily thinking:

Libre como el viento!

Free like the wind!

A woman at times must
choose to be a mother
or to keep her course.

To be a mother or not
to be...
Judge me if you may,
As women, we have now
that right
—To be conscious
mothers or no mothers
at all—.

EL MOLINO Y EL SUEÑO

By: Heidy Rodriguez

El día se presenta
como un caballero en su
fino semental
hermoso y lleno de
futuras memorias
promesas y flores

El molino amanece
con sus fieles
al maíz en su ritual
mañanero
mientras yo,
desperté a despedirme de
la vida
que conocí

El sueño llegó a mi vida
decide ir por aquello
lo desconocido
aquello
lo estremecedor
aquello que ya existío

El día de mi decisión
Armagedón

La batalla final entre
lo que fue y será

La tierra que sintió mi
primer palpitar,
la que me vio florecer
El atardecer que se
llevó consigo
mi primer amor,
illusión
Aquella feria patronal
que sintió mis pasos
Mi gozo y amor a la vida
a la cual esperaba como
una niña a su padre
trabajador.

Y así fue
como el cenzontle saluda
el alba,
Me desperté a dar un
canto de gloria
donde me despido del
molino
y a seguir mi sueño.

WE ARE DRAGONS

By: Veronica Lopez

I was not born and
raised to behave
and follow orders
Under the dictatorship
and patriarchy of
avaricious men,
I was not born to mold
myself to anyone's liking
or act accordingly,
I was put on this earth to
avenge history,
To avenge my fallen sisters
and ancestors before me,
Who were raped,
slaughtered, and
stolen from,
Who continue to be
put down and treated
like animals,
All at the mercy of white
hands, stained from
hundreds of years of blood.

I was not forged to fall
victim to silence and
make a home out of chains,
Like so many scream
at me to do.
I am a dragon, who comes
from a line of dragons
before me,
And we are not to be tamed,
ridden, and used as anyone
sees fit,
We are not to be
domesticated, muzzled, or
rid of our true nature,
We are born to fly, to bring
balance to the earth with
our fiery breath,
And to lay waste to
kingdoms with systems that
benefit us no more.

PEREGRINA MODERNA © (SOY MIGRANTE)

By: Sara Zapata Mijares

Soy migrante Yucateca
Hija de X-Zazil, madre
del mestizaje
Hija de Enrique y de
Felipa
De Tibolón y de Sotuta
Hija de maestra de Mama
y Muna
Hija del chiclero de la
selva Quintanarroense
Del alforzador de
guayaberas
Del beisbolista
Munense
Que hoy reposa
en Hoctún
Soy hija de la tierra
roja maya yucateca
Con olor a mar
de Progreso
A pescado fresco y
chile habanero
Con sabor a cochinita
pibil y relleno negro
Empanadas, panuchos
y salbutes,
Frutas de caimitos,
mamey y mandarinas.
Soy de color huaya y
amarillo X-kanlol
Soy hija de ceiba,
laureles y palmeras
Soy de la tierra de los
Dioses Mayas
Tierra del Faisán y
del Venado
De las pirámides de
Chichen Itzá y Uxmal
De cenotes con
entradas a inframundo
Donde la enseñanza
de mi abuelo
Dejo huella en
mi vuelo.
Soy de la ciudad
blanca y gentil
Del trovador
enamorado
Soy la novia de las
serenatas yucatecas
De la princesa de los
carnavales
Soy la que se fue y
el espíritu dejó.
Soy la peregrina
moderna
La que se fue detrás
del sueño americano

La que sueña con el
regreso mexicano
Soy de los muchos que
se fueron
De los pocos que
quedaron
De los muchos que se
quedaron
De los pocos que se
fueron
Soy la abuela, la
madre
La esposa, la hermana
La tía, la hija, la
prima,
La amiga, la vecina
La que se fue?
O la que se quedó?
Soy la peregrina
moderna
La del nuevo milenio
Soy la llamada
migrante
Esposa de guerrero
mexicano
Madre de hijos
amestizados y
aculturados.
Soy la Yucateca que
por sus venas
Corre sangre Maya
La que regresa
de turista
Con boleto regular
O en caja de ataúd
en cargo.

Soy aquella de la cual
mis descendientes,
Leerán de mí en los
libros de textos
La década entrante
Soy la peregrina
nostálgica
La peregrina moderna
La llamada migrante
Hija de brasero, de
regador de campo
Y piscador de frutas
Hermana de lavaplatos
y lava carros
De trabajador
de fábricas, de
alfombradores
De costureros y
algunos comerciantes
Los llamados
migrantes
Los del 3x1
Los del Dia del
Migrante Yucateco
Soy la peregrina
moderna
Soy la hija de Muna
Acuérdense de mí
Aunque sea una vez
por año
Soy maya Yucateca
Soy...la llamada
migrante.

Want to connect with
more LatinX Poets,

Let's connect at:

Instragram: @alegriamagazine
Facebook: Alegriamagazine
www.alegriamagazine.com